Vegetarian Recipes Cookbook for Beginners

The 30-Minute Vegetarian Breakfast Cookbook:
50 Healthy, Delicious Meals for Busy People

Amanda Altman

The following Book is reproduced below with the goal of providing information that is as accurate and reliable as possible. Regardless, purchasing this Book can be seen as consent to the fact that both the publisher and the author of this book are in no way experts on the topics discussed within and that any recommendations or suggestions that are made herein are for entertainment purposes only. Professionals should be consulted as needed prior to undertaking any of the action endorsed herein.

This declaration is deemed fair and valid by both the American Bar Association and the Committee of Publishers Association and is legally binding throughout the United States.

Furthermore, the transmission, duplication, or reproduction of any of the following work including specific information will be considered an illegal act irrespective of if it is done electronically or in print. This extends to creating a secondary or tertiary copy of the work or a recorded copy and is only allowed with the express written consent from the Publisher. All additional right reserved.

The information in the following pages is broadly considered a truthful and accurate account of facts and as such, any inattention, use, or misuse of the information in question by the reader will render any resulting actions solely under their purview. There are no scenarios in which the publisher or the original author of this work can be in any fashion deemed liable for any hardship or damages that may befall them after undertaking information described herein.

Additionally, the information in the following pages is intended only for informational purposes and should thus be thought of as universal. As befitting its nature, it is presented without assurance regarding its prolonged validity or interim quality. Trademarks that are mentioned are done without written consent and can in no way be considered an endorsement from the trademark holder.

Table of Content

Sommario

Introduction:

A meat-free diet can lead to better health for several reasons.

One reason is that many people who follow a vegetarian diet tend to consume a high proportion of fresh, healthful, plant-based foods, which provide antioxidants and fiber. When a person decides to follow a meat-free diet, they often become more active in making overall healthy choices.

Many studies agree that a vegetarian diet can offer a range of health benefits.

A vegetarian diet focuses on plants for food.

These include fruits, vegetables, dried beans and peas, grains, seeds and nuts.

People who follow vegetarian diets can get all the nutrients they need. However, they must be careful to eat a wide variety of foods to meet their nutritional needs. Nutrients vegetarians may need to focus on include protein, iron, calcium, zinc and vitamin B12.

1 - Breakfast Blackberry Bars

Preparation	Cooking	Servings
10 min	6 min	8

Ingredients:

- ½ cup grapeseed oil

- ¼ cup agave nectar

- 2 cups quinoa flakes

- 1 cup spelt flour

- ¼ teaspoon sea salt

- ½ cup blackberry fruits

- 4 baby bananas, ripe

Directions:

1.	Place the bananas, grapeseed oil, and agave. Stir and mash the banana until combined.

2.	Add the quinoa flakes and spelt flour into the bananas. Add the salt and blackberry last.

3.	Place the mixture in a parchment-lined bottom of the Instant Pot.

4.	Close the lid but do not set the vent to the Sealing position.

5.	Press the Slow Cook button and adjust the cooking time to 5 to 6 hours.

6.	Once cooked, allow to cool before removing and slicing into bars.

Nutrition: Calories per serving: 433 Protein: 9.9 g Carbs: 57.3 g Sugar: 10.5 g Fat: 19.7 g

2 - Alkaline Sausage Links

Preparation	Cooking	Servings
30 min	**5 min**	**6**

Ingredients:

- 2 cups garbanzos beans flour - 1 cup chopped mushrooms
- ½ cup chopped onions
- 1 tomato, chopped
- 1 teaspoon oregano
- 1 teaspoon sea salt

- 1 teaspoon ground sage
- 1 teaspoon dill, chopped
- ½ teaspoon cayenne pepper powder
- Grapeseed oil for frying

Directions:

1. Place all ingredients in a bowl except for the grapeseed oil.
2. Use your hands and mix all ingredients until well-combined.
3. Create small logs of sausages and place inside the fridge to set for at least 30 minutes.
4. Pour oil in the Instant Pot and press the Sauté button until the oil is hot.
5. Place the sausage links carefully and cook on all sides for 3 minutes.

Nutrition: Calories per serving: 266 Protein: 14.6 g Carbs: 44.9 g Sugar: 8.6 g Fat: 4.2 g

3 - Pumpkin Spice Quinoa

Preparation	Cooking	Servings
20 min		**4**

Ingredients:

- 1 cup cooked quinoa

- 1 cup unsweetened coconut milk

- 1 large banana, mashed

- ¼ cup pumpkin puree

- 1 teaspoon pumpkin spice

- 2 teaspoons chia seeds

Directions:

1. Mix all the ingredients in a container.
2. Seal the lid and shake well to mix.
3. Refrigerate overnight.
4. Serve.

Nutrition: Calories: 212Fat: 11.9 gCarbs: 31.7 gProtein: 7.3 gFiber: 2 g

4 - Teff Breakfast Porridge

Preparation	Cooking	Servings
5 min	**10 min**	**4**

Ingredients:

- ½ cup teff grain

- 2 cups spring water

- A pinch of sea salt

- ½ cup agave

- ¼ cup fresh blueberries

Directions:

1.   Place the teff grain and spring water in the Instant Pot. Stir in the sea salt.

2.   Close the lid and set the vent to the Sealing position.

3.   Press the Multigrain button and adjust the cooking time to 10 minutes. Cook on high.

4.   Once the timer sets off, do natural pressure release.

5.   Place the porridge in bowls and drizzle with agave. Top with blueberries.

Nutrition: Calories per serving: 105 Protein: 3.3 g Carbs: 21.8 g Sugar: 3.8 g Fat: 0.6 g

5 - Alkaline Blueberry and Strawberry Muffins

Preparation	Cooking	Servings
10 min	8 min	5

Ingredients:

- ¾ cup quinoa flour - ¾ cup teff flour

- ½ teaspoon salt - 1/3 cup agave

- 1 cup fresh coconut milk

- ¼ cup strawberries, chopped

- ¼ cup blueberries

Directions:

1. Place the quinoa flour, teff flour, and salt in a bowl.
2. In another bowl, combine the agave and coconut milk. Slowly pour the wet ingredients into the dry ingredients.
3. Mix until well-combined.
4. Stir in the berries and mix until well-combined.
5. Pour the batter in muffin pans.
6. Place the muffin pans with the batter in the Instant Pot.
7. Close the lid but do not set the vent to the Sealing position.
8. Press the Slow Cook button and adjust the cooking time to 4 to 5 hours.

Nutrition: Calories per serving: 271 Protein: 7.2 g Carbs: 36.6 g Sugar: 4.3 g Fat: 11.5 g

6 - Homefries Hashbrowns

Preparation	Cooking	Servings
6 min	**7 min**	**5**

Ingredients:

- 3 green bananas, peeled and chopped

- ¼ cup onion, diced

- ¼ cup green pepper, seeded and diced

- 1 plum tomato, diced

- 1 teaspoon sea salt

- 1 teaspoon oregano

- ½ teaspoon cayenne powder

- Grapeseed oil for frying

Directions:

1. Place all ingredients except for the grapeseed oil in a bowl. Mix until well-combined.
2. Press the Sauté button on the Instant Pot and heat the oil.
3. Get a tablespoon of the mixture and place it in the Instant Pot. Flatten to form a small pancake.
4. Cook for 3 minutes on all sides.
5. Do the same thing to the rest of the mixture.

Nutrition: Calories per serving: 77 Protein: 0.66 g Carbs: 13.4 g Sugar: 7.8 g Fat: 3 g

7 - Crustless Spinach Quiche

Preparation	Cooking	Servings
25 min	35 min	4

Ingredients:

- 2 teaspoons vegetable oil

- 5/8 onion, chopped

- 5/8 (10 ounce) package frozen chopped spinach, thawed and drained

- 3-1/4 eggs, beaten

- 1-2/3 cups and 1 tablespoon shredded Muenster cheese

- 1/8 teaspoon salt

- 1/8 teaspoon ground black pepper

Directions:

2. Preheat oven to 350 degrees F (175 degrees C). Lightly grease a 9 inch pie pan.

3. Heat oil in a large skillet over medium-high heat. Add onions and cook, stirring occasionally, until onions are soft. Stir in spinach and continue cooking until excess moisture has evaporated.

4. In a large bowl, combine eggs, cheese, salt and pepper. Add spinach mixture and stir to blend. Scoop into prepared pie pan.

5. Bake in preheated oven until eggs have set, about 30 minutes. Let cool for 10 minutes before serving.

Nutrition: Calories per serving: 310 calories; protein 20.4g; carbohydrates 4.8g; fat 23.7g; cholesterol 209.2mg; sodium 545.6mg.

8 - Gorgonzola Tofu Scramble

Preparation	Cooking	Servings
12 min	12 min	4

Ingredients:

- 3 tablespoons olive oil

- 5/8 (12 ounce) package extra-firm tofu, cut into cubes

- 1/2 cup chopped red onion

- 2 cloves garlic, minced

- 1-3/4 cups and 1 tablespoon sliced white mushrooms

- 2 cups packed fresh spinach

- 1/4 cup and 2 tablespoons crumbled Gorgonzola cheese

Directions:

1. Heat olive oil in a skillet over medium heat; cook and stir tofu, onion, and garlic until onion is translucent, 5 to 10 minutes. Add mushrooms; cook and stir until mushrooms are tender and tofu is lightly browned, 5 to 10 minutes.

2. Remove skillet from heat. Mix spinach and Gorgonzola cheese into tofu mixture until spinach begins to wilt and the cheese melts from the heat of the tofu mixture.

Nutrition: Calories per serving: 210 calories; protein 9.7g; carbohydrates 5.1g; fat 17.5g; cholesterol 17mg; sodium 177.5mg.

9 - Chakchouka

Preparation	Cooking	Servings
25 min	**25 min**	**4**

Ingredients:

- 3 tablespoons olive oil

- 1 ⅓ cups chopped onion

- 1 cup thinly sliced bell peppers, any color

- 2 cloves garlic, minced, or to taste

- 2 ½ cups chopped tomatoes

- 1 teaspoon ground cumin

- 1 teaspoon paprika

- 1 teaspoon salt

- 1 hot chile pepper, seeded and finely chopped, or to taste

- 4 eggs

Directions:

1. Heat the olive oil in a skillet over medium heat. Stir in the onion, bell peppers, and garlic; cook and stir until the vegetables have softened and the onion has turned translucent, about 5 minutes.

2. Combine the tomatoes, cumin, paprika, salt, and chile pepper into a bowl and mix briefly. Pour the tomato mixture into the skillet, and stir to combine.

3. Simmer, uncovered, until the tomato juices have cooked off, about 10 minutes.

Make four indentations in the tomato mixture for the eggs. Crack the eggs into the indentations. Cover the skillet and let the eggs cook until they're firm but not dry, about 5 minutes.

Nutrition: Calories per serving: 209 calories; protein 7.8g; carbohydrates 12.9g; fat 15g; cholesterol 163.7mg; sodium 653.7mg.

10 - Easy Broccoli Quiche

Preparation	Cooking	Servings
25 min	**35 min**	4

Ingredients:

- 5/8 (9 inch) unbaked pie crust

- 2 teaspoons butter, melted

- 5/8 onion, minced

- 3/4 teaspoon minced garlic

- 1-1/3 cups chopped fresh broccoli

- 1 cup shredded mozzarella cheese

- 2-3/4 eggs, well beaten

- 1 cup milk

- 3/4 teaspoon salt

- 1/4 teaspoon black pepper

- 2 teaspoons butter, melted

Directions:

1.   Preheat oven to 350 degrees F (175 degrees C). Line a 9-inch deep-dish pie pan with crust.

2.   Melt 2 tablespoons butter in a large saucepan over medium-low heat. Add onion, garlic, and broccoli. Cook slowly, stirring occasionally, until vegetables are soft. Spoon vegetables into crust and sprinkle with cheese.

3.   Combine eggs and milk. Season with salt and pepper. Stir in remaining 1 tablespoon

melted butter. Pour egg mixture over vegetables and cheese.

4.   Bake in preheated oven until center has set, 30 to 50 minutes.

Nutrition: Calories per serving: 388 calories; protein 16.1g; carbohydrates 21.5g; fat 26.8g; cholesterol 167.3mg; sodium 898.2mg.

11 - Baby Spinach Omelet

Preparation	Cooking	Servings
10 min	10 min	4

Ingredients:

- 8 eggs

- 4 cups torn baby spinach leaves

- 1/4 cup and 2 teaspoons grated Parmesan cheese

- 1 teaspoon onion powder

- 1/2 teaspoon ground nutmeg

- salt and pepper to taste

Directions:

1.   In a bowl, beat the eggs, and stir in the baby spinach and Parmesan cheese. Season with onion powder, nutmeg, salt, and pepper.

2.   In a small skillet coated with cooking spray over medium heat, cook the egg mixture about 3 minutes, until partially set. Flip with a spatula, and continue cooking 2 to 3 minutes. Reduce heat to low, and continue cooking 2 to 3 minutes, or to desired doneness.

Nutrition: Calories per serving: 186 calories; protein 16.4g; carbohydrates 2.8g; fat 12.3g; cholesterol 378.6mg; sodium 278.7mg.

12 - Vegan Pancakes

Preparation	Cooking	Servings
9 min	12 min	4

Ingredients:

- 1-2/3 cups all-purpose flour

- 2 tablespoons and 2 teaspoons white sugar

- 2-3/4 teaspoons baking powder

- 3/4 teaspoon salt

- 1-2/3 cups water

- 1 tablespoon and 1 teaspoon oil

Directions:

1.   Sift the flour, sugar, baking powder, and salt into a large bowl. Whisk the water and oil together in a small bowl. Make a well in the center of the dry ingredients, and pour in the wet. Stir just until blended; mixture will be lumpy.

2.   Heat a lightly oiled griddle over medium-high heat. Drop batter by large spoonfuls onto the griddle, and cook until bubbles form and the edges are dry. Flip, and cook until browned on the other side. Repeat with remaining batter.

Nutrition: Calories per serving: 264 calories; protein 5.4g; carbohydrates 48.9g; fat 5.1g; sodium 716.7mg.

13 - Egg White Breakfast Bites

Preparation	Cooking	Servings
18 min	**20 min**	4

Ingredients:

- cooking spray

- 3/8 (16 ounce) carton liquid egg whites

- 2 tablespoons and 2 teaspoons low-fat cottage cheese

- 1/8 teaspoon garlic powder

- 1/8 teaspoon salt

- 1/8 teaspoon ground black pepper

- 1/3 cup packed fresh spinach, finely chopped

- 1 tablespoon and 2-1/4 teaspoons roasted red peppers, drained and chopped

- 1 teaspoon fresh basil, minced

- 2 tablespoons and 3/4 teaspoon crumbled feta cheese

Directions:

1. Preheat the oven to 350 degrees F (175 degrees C). Spray a 12-cup muffin pan generously with cooking spray.

2. Combine egg whites, cottage cheese, garlic powder, salt, and pepper in a blender; blend until smooth, about 15 seconds.

3. Combine spinach, roasted red peppers, and basil in a bowl. Pour in egg mixture and stir to combine. Ladle the mixture evenly into the muffin cups, filling each

about 3/4 full. Top each muffin with 1 teaspoon feta cheese.

4.   Bake in the preheated oven until egg white bites are set, 18 to 20 minutes.

Nutrition: Calories per serving: 57 calories; protein 6.7g; carbohydrates 1.3g; fat 2.6g; cholesterol 5.8mg; sodium 236mg.

14 - German Potato Pancakes

Preparation	Cooking	Servings
30 min	7 min	6

Ingredients:

- 2 eggs

- 2 tablespoons all-purpose flour

- 1/4 teaspoon baking powder

- 1/2 teaspoon salt

- 1/4 teaspoon pepper

- 6 medium potatoes, peeled and shredded

- 1/2 cup finely chopped onion

- 1/4 cup vegetable oil

Directions:

In a large bowl, beat together eggs, flour, baking powder, salt, and pepper. Mix in potatoes and onion.

Heat oil in a large skillet over medium heat. In batches, drop heaping tablespoonfuls of the potato mixture into the skillet. Press to flatten. Cook about 3 minutes on each side, until browned and crisp. Drain on paper towels.

Nutrition: Calories per serving: 283 calories; protein 6.8g; carbohydrates 40.7g; fat 11g; cholesterol 62mg; sodium 245.5mg.

15 - Turkish Eggs (Cilbir)

Preparation	Cooking	Servings
30 min	15 min	4

Ingredients For the Yogurt Spread:

- 2 cups Greek yogurt, at room temperature

- 2 cloves garlic

- 1/2 teaspoon salt, or to taste

- 1 teaspoon freshly ground black pepper

- 2 pinches cayenne pepper

- 1/2 cup and 2 tablespoons finely chopped fresh dill, or to taste

Ingredient For the Aleppo Butter:

- ½ stick unsalted butter
- ¼ teaspoon ground cumin
- ½ teaspoon smoked paprika
- 1 tablespoon Aleppo chili flakes

Ingredient For the Optional Parsley and Jalapeno Oil:

- 1 tablespoon chopped fresh parsley
- 1 tablespoon diced jalapeno pepper
- 1/2 teaspoon salt, or to taste
- 2 tablespoons olive oil (Optional)

Ingredient For the Rest:

- 1 tablespoon white vinegar, or as needed
- 4 large eggs
- 1 pinch sea salt

Directions:

1. Spoon yogurt into a medium bowl. Grate in garlic and mix to combine. Season with salt, pepper, and cayenne. Add dill and mix thoroughly. Set aside at room temperature.

2. Melt butter in a saucepan over medium heat; heat until bubbles begin to burst. Add cumin, paprika, and chili flakes. Stir until color is uniform, then turn off heat and let spices infuse.

3. Grind parsley and jalapeno together in a mortar. Season with salt, drizzle in olive oil, and stir to combine.

4. Fill a large saucepan with 2 to 3 inches of water and bring to a boil. Reduce heat to medium-low, pour in vinegar, and keep the water at a gentle simmer. Crack an egg into a small bowl then gently slip egg into the simmering water, holding the bowl just above the surface of water. Repeat with the remaining eggs. Cook eggs until the whites are firm and the yolks have thickened but are not hard, 2 1/2 to 3

minutes. Remove the eggs from the water with a slotted spoon, dab on a kitchen towel to remove excess water, and place onto a warm plate.

5.	Dollop yogurt mixture onto serving plates. Use the back of a spoon to spread yogurt out into a bed for the eggs, carving ridges into the top to catch the oil. Drizzle on some jalapeno oil. Top with eggs and a spoonful or two of the Aleppo butter. Sprinkle sea salt on top.

Nutrition: Calories per serving: 616 calories; protein 19.9g; carbohydrates 8.6g; fat 57.1g; cholesterol 455.5mg; sodium 742.8mg.

16 - Spinach Mushroom Quiche

Preparation	Cooking	Servings
20 min	**50 min**	**6**

Ingredients:

- 1 prepared 9-inch single pie crust

- 4 eggs

- ¾ cup milk

- 1 tablespoon chopped fresh parsley

- 1 teaspoon minced garlic

- ½ teaspoon salt

- ½ teaspoon ground black pepper

- ⅛ teaspoon ground nutmeg

- ½ (10 ounce) bag fresh spinach

- 1 (8 ounce) package sliced fresh mushrooms

- ½ yellow onion, sliced

- ½ (4 ounce) container crumbled feta cheese

- ½ (8 ounce) package shredded Swiss cheese, divided

Directions:

1. Preheat oven to 400 degrees F (200 degrees C).

2. Fit pie crust into a 9-inch pie dish.

3. Whisk eggs, milk, parsley, garlic, salt, black pepper, and nutmeg in a bowl.

4. Gently combine spinach, mushrooms, onion, and feta cheese in a separate bowl.

Spread spinach-mushroom mixture in the prepared pie dish; top with half the Swiss cheese.

5. Pour egg mixture evenly over the filling, swirling egg mixture in bowl to spread seasonings through the eggs; top the quiche with remaining Swiss cheese. Place quiche on a baking sheet.

6. Bake in preheated oven until the quiche is lightly puffed and browned, 45 to 50 minutes. A toothpick inserted into the center of the filling should come out clean. Cool for 30 minutes before serving.

Nutrition: Calories per serving: 334 calories; protein 15.6g; carbohydrates 21g; fat 21.4g; cholesterol 152.2mg; sodium 572.1mg.

17 - Spinach Quiche

Preparation	Cooking	Servings
30 min	55 min	6

Ingredients:

- ½ cup light mayonnaise

- ½ cup milk

- 4 eggs, lightly beaten

- 8 ounces shredded reduced-fat Cheddar cheese

- 1 (10 ounce) package frozen chopped spinach, thawed and squeezed dry

- ¼ cup chopped onion

- 1 (9 inch) unbaked pie shell

Directions:

1. Preheat oven to 400 degrees F (200 degrees C). Line a cookie sheet with foil.

2. In a large bowl, whisk together mayonnaise and milk until smooth. Whisk in eggs. Layer spinach, cheese, and onion in pie shell, making several layers of each. Pour in egg mixture. Place quiche on prepared cookie sheet. Cover quiche with foil.

3. Bake in preheated oven for 45 minutes. Remove cover, and bake 10 to 15 minutes, or until top is golden brown and filling is set.

Nutrition: Calories per serving: 356 calories; protein 17.9g; carbohydrates 19.9g; fat 23.2g; cholesterol 140.6mg; sodium 612.1mg.

18 - Home-Fried Potatoes

Preparation	Cooking	Servings
25 min	**30 min**	**4**

Ingredients:

- 4 red potatoes

- 1 tablespoon olive oil

- 1 onion, chopped

- 1 green bell pepper, seeded and chopped

- 2 tablespoons olive oil

- 1 teaspoon salt

- ¾ teaspoon paprika

- ¼ teaspoon ground black pepper

- ¼ cup chopped fresh parsley

Directions:

1. Bring a large pot of salted water to a boil. Add potatoes and cook until tender but still firm, about 15 minutes. Drain, cool cut into 1/2 inch cubes.

2. In a large skillet, heat 1 tablespoon olive oil over medium high heat. Add onion and green pepper. Cook, stirring often, until soft; about 5 minutes. Transfer to a plate and set aside.

3. Pour remaining 2 tablespoons of oil into the skillet and turn heat to medium-high. Add potato cubes, salt, paprika and black pepper. Cook, stirring occasionally, until potatoes are browned; about 10 minutes. Stir in the onions, green peppers and

parsley and cook for another minute. Serve hot.

Nutrition: Calories per serving: 262 calories; protein 4.7g; carbohydrates 38.3g; fat 10.6g; sodium 601.6mg.

19 - Homemade Hashbrowns

Preparation	Cooking	Servings
10 min	**10 min**	**4**

Ingredients:

- 2 cups mashed potatoes

- 1 egg, beaten

- 1 onion, finely diced

- ½ teaspoon salt

- ¼ teaspoon ground black pepper

- 2 tablespoons olive oil

Directions:

1. Beat egg in a medium size mixing bowl. Mix egg and onion with mashed potatoes. Add salt and pepper.

2. Heat olive oil in a medium size frying pan, over a medium heat. Scoop the potato mixutre into the frying pan in 4 inch circles, pat with a spatula to flatten the mounds to approximately 1/2 to 1 inch thick. Cook until bottom is browned. Flip the patty over and brown on the other side.

Nutrition: Calories per serving: 176 calories; protein 3.9g; carbohydrates 21.2g; fat 8.6g; cholesterol 48.6mg; sodium 626.6mg.

20 - Veggie Omelet

Preparation	Cooking	Servings
10 min	10 min	4

Ingredients:

- 2 tablespoons butter

- 1 small onion, chopped

- 1 green bell pepper, chopped

- 4 eggs

- 2 tablespoons milk

- ¾ teaspoon salt

- ⅛ teaspoon freshly ground black pepper

- 2 ounces shredded Swiss cheese

Directions:

1. Melt one tablespoon butter in a medium skillet over medium heat. Place onion and bell pepper inside of the skillet. Cook for 4 to 5 minutes stirring occasionally until vegetables are just tender.

2. While the vegetables are cooking beat the eggs with the milk, 1/2 teaspoon salt and pepper.

3. Shred the cheese into a small bowl and set it aside.

4. Remove the vegetables from heat, transfer them to another bowl and sprinkle the remaining 1/4 teaspoon salt over them.

5.   Melt the remaining 1 tablespoon butter (in the skillet just used to cook the vegetables) over medium heat. Coat the skillet with the butter. When the butter is bubbly add the egg mixture and cook the egg for 2 minutes or until the eggs begin to set on the bottom of the pan. Gently lift the edges of the omelet with a spatula to let the uncooked part of the eggs flow toward the edges and cook. Continue cooking for 2 to 3 minutes or until the center of the omelet starts to look dry.

6.   Sprinkle the cheese over the omelet and spoon the vegetable mixture into the center of the omelet. Using a spatula gently fold one edge of the omelet over the vegetables. Let the omelet cook for another two minutes or until the cheese melts to your desired consistency. Slide the omelet out of the skillet and onto a plate. Cut in half and serve.

Nutrition: Calories per serving: 386 calories; protein 21.7g; carbohydrates 9.1g; fat 29.8g; cholesterol 429.8mg; sodium 1157.8mg.

21 - Cornmeal Mush

Preparation	Cooking	Servings
8 min	10 min	8

Ingredients:

- 1 ¼ cups cornmeal

- 2 ½ cups water

- ½ teaspoon salt

Directions:

1.   Mix together cornmeal, water, and salt in a medium saucepan. Cook over medium heat, stirring frequently, until mixture thickens, about 5 to 7 minutes.

2.   If using as cereal, spoon mush into bowls and serve with milk and sugar, if desired. If frying, pour mixture into a loaf pan and chill completely. Remove from pan, cut into slices, and fry in a small amount of oil over medium-high heat until browned on both sides. Serve with sauce of your choice.

Nutrition: Calories per serving: 80 calories; protein 1.6g; carbohydrates 17.1g; fat 0.4g; sodium 146.9mg.

22 - Tofu Burrito Bowls

Preparation	Cooking	Servings
20 min	35 min	4

Ingredients:

- 1 tablespoon and 1 teaspoon olive oil

- 1-1/4 (14 ounce) packages extra-firm tofu, drained

- 3/4 teaspoon salt

- black pepper to taste

- 2 teaspoons onion powder

- 2 teaspoons garlic powder

- 1/8 teaspoon ground turmeric

- 1-1/2 teaspoons fresh lemon juice

- 1 tablespoon and 1 teaspoon olive oil

- 1-1/3 cups finely diced red onion

- 2-3/4 jalapeno peppers, seeded and chopped

- 3/4 teaspoon salt

- 4 cloves garlic, minced

- 3-1/4 cups chopped tomatoes

- 2 teaspoons cumin

- 1/3 cup chopped fresh cilantro

- 1-1/2 teaspoons fresh lemon juice

- 1-1/4 (15.5 ounce) cans no-salt-added black beans, drained and rinsed

- 3-1/4 cups cooked hash brown potatoes

- 1-1/4 avocado - peeled, pitted and sliced

- 1-1/2 teaspoons fresh lemon juice

- 1/3 cup chopped fresh cilantro

- 1-1/4 teaspoons hot sauce, or to taste

Directions:

1. Preheat a large, heavy skillet over medium-high heat. Add 2 tablespoons oil. Break tofu apart over skillet into bite-size pieces, sprinkle with salt and pepper, then cook, stirring frequently with a thin metal spatula, until liquid cooks out and tofu browns, about 10 minutes. (If you notice liquid collecting in pan, increase heat to evaporate water.) Be sure to get under the tofu when you stir, scraping the bottom of the pan where the good, crispy stuff is and keeping it from sticking.

2. Add onion and garlic powders, turmeric, juice, and remaining tablespoon oil and toss to coat. Cook 5 minutes more.

3.   Preheat a heavy-bottomed saucepan over medium-high heat. Add oil. Cook onion and jalapenos with a pinch of salt, stirring, until translucent, about 5 minutes, Add garlic and cook, stirring, until fragrant, about 30 seconds. Add tomatoes, cumin, and remaining salt, and cook, stirring, until tomatoes become saucy, about 5 minutes. Add cilantro and lemon juice. Let cilantro wilt in. Add beans and heat through, stirring occasionally, about 2 minutes. Taste for salt and seasoning.

4.   Spoon some hash browns into each bowl, followed by a scoop of beans and a scoop of scramble. Top with avocado, a squeeze of fresh lemon juice, and a sprinkle of cilantro. Serve with hot sauce.

Nutrition: Calories per serving: 579 calories; protein 22g; carbohydrates 57.2g; fat 39.6g; sodium 1170.5mg.

23 - Green Smoothie Bowl

Preparation	Cooking	Servings
12 min	12 min	4

Ingredients:

- 6 cups fresh spinach

- 2 banana

- 1 (14 ounce) can coconut milk

- 1 cup frozen mango chunks

- 1 cup coconut water

Toppings:

- ⅓ cup fresh raspberries
- ¼ cup fresh blueberries
- 2 tablespoons granola
- 1 tablespoon coconut flakes
- ¼ teaspoon sliced almonds
- ¼ teaspoon chia seeds

Directions:

1. Blend spinach, banana, coconut milk, mango, and coconut water in a blender until smooth. Pour smoothie into a bowl and top with raspberries, blueberries, granola, coconut flakes, almonds, and chia seeds.

Nutrition: Calories per serving: 374 calories; protein 6.3g; carbohydrates 37g; fat 25.6g; sodium 115.9mg.

24 - Quinoa Porridge

Preparation	Cooking	Servings
10 min	35 min	4

Ingredients:

- 2/3 cup quinoa

- 1/4 teaspoon ground cinnamon

- 2 cups almond milk

- 2/3 cup water

- 2 tablespoons and 1-3/4 teaspoons brown sugar

- 1-1/4 teaspoons vanilla extract

- 1-1/4 pinches salt

Directions:

2. Heat a saucepan over medium heat and measure in the quinoa. Season with cinnamon and cook until toasted, stirring frequently, about 3 minutes. Pour in the almond milk, water and vanilla and stir in the brown sugar and salt. Bring to a boil, then cook over low heat until the porridge is thick and grains are tender, about 25 minutes. Add more water if needed if the liquid has dried up before it finishes cooking. Stir occasionally, especially at the end, to prevent burning.

Nutrition: Calories per serving: 173 calories; protein 4.3g; carbohydrates 31.3g; fat 3g; sodium 89.7mg.

25 - Tomato and Basil Quiche

Preparation	Cooking	Servings
25 min	**45 min**	**6**

Ingredients:

- 1 tablespoon olive oil

- 1 onion, sliced

- 2 tomatoes, peeled and sliced

- 2 tablespoons all-purpose flour

- 2 teaspoons dried basil

- 3 eggs, beaten

- ½ cup milk

- salt and pepper to taste

- 1 (9 inch) unbaked deep dish pie crust

- 1 ½ cups shredded Colby-Monterey Jack cheese, divided

Directions:

3. Preheat oven to 400 degrees F (200 degrees C). Bake pie shell in preheated oven for 8 minutes.

4. Meanwhile, heat olive oil in a large skillet over medium heat. Saute onion until soft; remove from skillet. Sprinkle tomato slices with flour and basil, then saute 1 minute on each side. In a small bowl, whisk together eggs and milk. season with salt and pepper.

5. Spread 1 cup shredded cheese in the bottom of pie crust. Layer onions over cheese, and top with tomatoes. Cover with egg mixture. sprinkle top with remaining 1/2 cup shredded cheese.

6. Bake in preheated oven for 10 minutes. Reduce heat to 350 degrees F (175 degrees C), and bake for 15 to 20 minutes, or until filling is puffed and golden brown. Serve warm.

Nutrition: Calories per serving: 379 calories; protein 13.7g; carbohydrates 23g; fat 26.1g; cholesterol 127.3mg; sodium 697.5mg.

26 - Autumn Apple Salad

Preparation	Cooking	Servings
15 min	15 min	4

Ingredients:

- 4 tart green apples, cored and chopped

- ¼ cup blanched slivered almonds, toasted

- ¼ cup dried cranberries

- ¼ cup chopped dried cherries

- 1 (8 ounce) container vanilla yogurt

Directions:

In a medium bowl, stir together the apples, almonds, cranberries, cherries and yogurt until evenly coated.

Nutrition: Calories per serving: 202 calories; protein 5.1g; carbohydrates 38.9g; fat 4.1g; cholesterol 2.8mg; sodium 40.8mg.

27 - California Grilled Veggie Sandwich

Preparation	Cooking	Servings
35 min	25 min	4

Ingredients:

- ¼ cup mayonnaise

- 3 cloves garlic, minced

- 1 tablespoon lemon juice

- ⅛ cup olive oil

- 1 cup sliced red bell peppers

- 1 small zucchini, sliced

- 1 red onion, sliced

- 1 small yellow squash, sliced

- 2 (4-x6-inch) focaccia bread pieces, split horizontally

- ½ cup crumbled feta cheese

Directions:

1. In a bowl, mix the mayonnaise, minced garlic, and lemon juice. Set aside in the refrigerator.

2. Preheat the grill for high heat.

3. Brush vegetables with olive oil on each side. Brush grate with oil. Place bell peppers and zucchini closest to the middle of the grill, and set onion and squash pieces around them. Cook for about 3 minutes, turn, and cook for another 3 minutes. The peppers may take a bit longer. Remove from grill, and set aside.

4.   Spread some of the mayonnaise mixture on the cut sides of the bread, and sprinkle each one with feta cheese. Place on the grill cheese side up, and cover with lid for 2 to 3 minutes. This will warm the bread, and slightly melt the cheese. Watch carefully so the bottoms don't burn. Remove from grill, and layer with the vegetables. Enjoy as open faced grilled sandwiches.

Nutrition: Calories per serving: 393 calories; protein 9.2g; carbohydrates 36.5g; fat 23.8g; cholesterol 21.9mg; sodium 623.4mg.

28 - Roasted Vegetables

Preparation	Cooking	Servings
20 min	**45 min**	**10**

Ingredients:

- 1 small butternut squash, cubed

- 2 red bell peppers, seeded and diced

- 1 sweet potato, peeled and cubed

- 3 Yukon Gold potatoes, cubed

- 1 red onion, quartered

- 1 tablespoon chopped fresh thyme

- 2 tablespoons chopped fresh rosemary

- 1/4 cup olive oil

- 2 tablespoons balsamic vinegar

- salt and freshly ground black pepper

Directions:

Preheat oven to 475 degrees F (245 degrees C).

In a large bowl, combine the squash, red bell peppers, sweet potato, and Yukon Gold potatoes. Separate the red onion quarters into pieces, and add them to the mixture.

In a small bowl, stir together thyme, rosemary, olive oil, vinegar, salt, and pepper. Toss with vegetables until they are coated. Spread evenly on a large roasting pan.

Roast for 35 to 40 minutes in the preheated oven, stirring every 10 minutes, or until vegetables are cooked through and browned.

Nutrition: Calories per serving: 123 calories; protein 2g; carbohydrates 20g; fat 4.7g; sodium 26mg.

29 - Vegetable Soup

Preparation	Cooking	Servings
20 min	**30 min**	**6**

Ingredients:

- 1 (14 ounce) can chicken broth

- 1 (11.5 ounce) can tomato-vegetable juice cocktail

- 1 cup water

- 1 large potato, diced

- 2 carrots, sliced

- 2 stalks celery, diced

- 1 (14.5 ounce) can diced tomatoes

- 1 cup chopped fresh green beans

- 1 cup fresh corn kernels

- salt and pepper to taste

- Creole seasoning to taste

Directions:

1. In a large stock pot, combine broth, tomato juice, water, potatoes, carrots, celery, undrained chopped tomatoes, green beans, and corn. Season with salt, pepper and Creole seasoning. Bring to a boil and simmer for 30 minutes or until all vegetables are tender.

Nutrition: Calories per serving: 116 calories; protein 4g; carbohydrates 24.3g; fat 0.6g; cholesterol 1.6mg; sodium 639.5mg.

30 - Veggie Pizza

Preparation	Cooking	Servings
30 min	120 min	16

Ingredients:

- 2 (8 ounce) packages refrigerated crescent rolls

- 1 cup sour cream

- 1 (8 ounce) package cream cheese, softened

- 1 teaspoon dried dill weed

- ¼ teaspoon garlic salt

- 1 (1 ounce) package ranch dressing mix

- 1 small onion, finely chopped

- 1 stalk celery, thinly sliced

- ½ cup halved and thinly-sliced radishes

- 1 red bell pepper, chopped

- 1 ½ cups fresh broccoli, chopped

- 1 carrot, grated

Directions:

2. Preheat oven to 350 degrees F (175 degrees C). Spray a jellyroll pan with non-stick cooking spray.

3. Pat crescent roll dough into a jellyroll pan. Let stand 5 minutes. Pierce with fork.

4. Bake for 10 minutes, let cool.

5. In a medium-sized mixing bowl, combine sour cream, cream cheese, dill weed, garlic salt and ranch dip mix. Spread this mixture on top of the cooled crust. Arrange the onion, carrot, celery, broccoli,

radish, bell pepper and broccoli on top of the creamed mixture. Cover and let chill. Once chilled, cut it into squares and serve.

Nutrition: Calories per serving: 196 calories; protein 4.8g; carbohydrates 16g; fat 12.6g; cholesterol 35.7mg; sodium 358.6mg.

31 - Italian Vegetable Soup

Preparation	Cooking	Servings
25 min	**55 min**	**8**

Ingredients:

- 1 cup chopped onion

- 1 cup chopped celery

- 1 cup chopped carrots

- 2 cloves garlic, minced

- 1 (14.5 ounce) can peeled and diced tomatoes

- 1 (15 ounce) can tomato sauce

- 2 (19 ounce) cans kidney beans, drained and rinsed

- 2 cups water

- 5 teaspoons beef bouillon granules

- 1 tablespoon dried parsley

- ½ teaspoon dried oregano

- ½ teaspoon dried basil

- 2 cups chopped cabbage

- 1 (15.25 ounce) can whole kernel corn

- 1 (15 ounce) can green beans

- 1 cup macaroni

Directions:

1. Stir in onion, celery, carrots, garlic, chopped tomatoes, tomato sauce, beans, water and bouillon. Season with parsley, oregano and basil. Simmer for 20 minutes.

2.   Stir in cabbage, corn, green beans and pasta. Bring to a boil, then reduce heat. Simmer until vegetables are tender and pasta is al dente. Add more water if needed.

Nutrition: Calories per serving: 441 calories; protein 22.4g; carbohydrates 52.5g; fat 16.6g; cholesterol 48.4mg; sodium 1295mg

32 - Mexican Bean Salad

Preparation	Cooking	Servings
20 min		**8**

Ingredients:

- 1 (15 ounce) can black beans, rinsed and drained

- 1 (15 ounce) can kidney beans, drained

- 1 (15 ounce) can cannellini beans, drained and rinsed

- 1 green bell pepper, chopped

- 1 red bell pepper, chopped

- 1 (10 ounce) package frozen corn kernels

- 1 red onion, chopped

- ½ cup olive oil

- ½ cup red wine vinegar

- 2 tablespoons fresh lime juice

- 1 tablespoon lemon juice

- 2 tablespoons white sugar

- 1 tablespoon salt

- 1 clove crushed garlic

- ¼ cup chopped fresh cilantro

- ½ tablespoon ground cumin

- ½ tablespoon ground black pepper

- 1 dash hot pepper sauce

- ½ teaspoon chili powder

Directions:

1.   In a large bowl, combine beans, bell peppers, frozen corn, and red onion.

2.   In a small bowl, whisk together olive oil, red wine vinegar, lime juice, lemon juice, sugar, salt, garlic, cilantro, cumin, and black pepper. Season to taste with hot sauce and chili powder.

3.   Pour olive oil dressing over vegetables; mix well. Chill thoroughly, and serve cold.

Nutrition: Calories per serving: 334 calories; protein 11.2g; carbohydrates 41.7g; fat 14.8g; sodium 1158.8mg.

33 - Banana Bread

Preparation	Cooking	Servings
15 min	55 min	10

Ingredients:

- 3 ripe bananas, mashed
- 1 cup white sugar
- 1 egg
- ¼ cup melted butter
- 1 ½ cups all-purpose flour
- 1 teaspoon baking soda

- 1 teaspoon salt

Directions:

1. Preheat oven to 325 degrees F (165 degrees C). Grease a 9x5-inch loaf pan.

2. Combine bananas, sugar, egg, and butter together in a bowl. Mix flour and baking soda together in a separate bowl; stir into banana mixture until batter is just mixed. Stir salt into batter. Pour batter into the prepared loaf pan.

3. Bake in the preheated oven until a toothpick inserted in the center of the bread comes out clean, about 1 hour.

Nutrition: Calories per serving: 225 calories; protein 3g; carbohydrates 42.4g; fat 5.4g; cholesterol 30.8mg; sodium 398.8mg.

34 - German Potato Pancakes

Preparation	Cooking	Servings
30 min	10 min	6

Ingredients:

- 2 eggs

- 2 tablespoons all-purpose flour

- ¼ teaspoon baking powder

- ½ teaspoon salt

- ¼ teaspoon pepper

- 6 medium potatoes, peeled and shredded

- ½ cup finely chopped onion

- ¼ cup vegetable oil

Directions:

1.   In a large bowl, beat together eggs, flour, baking powder, salt, and pepper. Mix in potatoes and onion.

2.   Heat oil in a large skillet over medium heat. In batches, drop heaping tablespoonfuls of the potato mixture into the skillet. Press to flatten. Cook about 3 minutes on each side, until browned and crisp. Drain on paper towels.

Nutrition: Calories per serving: 283 calories; protein 6.8g; carbohydrates 40.7g; fat 11g; cholesterol 62mg; sodium 245.5mg.

35 - Avocado Toast

Preparation	Cooking	Servings
15 min		4

Ingredients:

- 4 slices whole-grain bread
- 1 avocado, halved and pitted
- 2 tablespoons chopped fresh parsley
- 1 ½ teaspoons extra-virgin olive oil
- ½ lemon, juiced
- ½ teaspoon salt

- ½ teaspoon ground black pepper
- ½ teaspoon onion powder
- ½ teaspoon garlic powder

Directions:

1. Toast bread in a toaster or toaster oven.

2. Scoop avocado into a bowl. Add parsley, olive oil, lemon juice, salt, pepper, onion powder, and garlic powder; mash together using a potato masher. Spread avocado mixture into each piece of toast.

Nutrition: Calories per serving: 170 calories; protein 4.9g; carbohydrates 16.8g; fat 10.1g; sodium 429.6mg.

36 - Veggie Griddle Cakes

Preparation	Cooking	Servings
15 min	15 min	4

Ingredients:

- 4 eggs
- 1 cup vanilla fat-free yogurt
- 2-1/2 cups biscuit baking mix
- 2 tablespoons vegetable oil
- 2 onion, diced
- 1 cup chopped green bell pepper

- 1 cup chopped red bell pepper
- 2 teaspoons chopped fresh parsley
- 2 small tomato, diced

Directions:

1. In a medium bowl blend eggs, yogurt and biscuit baking mix.

2. Heat oil in a medium skillet over medium heat. Saute onion, green bell pepper and red bell pepper, until tender; stir into batter.

3. Heat a lightly oiled griddle or frying pan over medium high heat. Pour or scoop the batter onto the griddle, using approximately 1/4 cup for each pancake. Brown on both sides and serve hot, garnished with parsley and tomatoes.

Nutrition: Calories per serving: 543 calories; protein 16.5g; carbohydrates 68.7g; fat 23.6g; cholesterol 187mg; sodium 1062.4mg.

37 - Greek Scrambled Eggs

Preparation	Cooking	Servings
10 min	10 min	4

Ingredients:

- 2 tablespoons butter
- 6 eggs
- 2 teaspoons water
- 1 cup crumbled feta cheese
- salt and pepper to taste

Directions:

1.   Heat butter in a skillet over medium-high heat. Beat eggs and water together, then pour into pan. Add feta cheese, and cook, stirring occasionally to scramble. Season with salt and pepper.

Nutrition: Calories per serving: 257 calories; protein 14.8g; carbohydrates 2.1g; fat 21.2g; cholesterol 327.6mg; sodium 709.7mg.

38 - Vanilla Crepes

Preparation	Cooking	Servings
10 min	10 min	12

Ingredients:

- 1 ½ cups milk

- 3 egg yolks

- 2 tablespoons vanilla extract

- 1 ½ cups all-purpose flour

- 2 tablespoons sugar

- ½ teaspoon salt

- 5 tablespoons melted butter

Directions:

2. In a large bowl, mix together the milk, egg yolks and vanilla. Stir in the flour, sugar, salt and melted butter until well blended.

3. Heat a crepe pan over medium heat until hot. Coat with vegetable oil or cooking spray. Pour about 1/4 cup of batter into the pan and tip to spread the batter to the edges. When bubbles form on the top and the edges are dry, flip over and cook until lightly browned on the other side and edges are golden. Repeat with remaining batter.

4. Fill crepes with your favorite fruit, cream, caramel or even ice cream or cheese to serve.

Nutrition: Calories per serving: 142 calories; protein 3.3g; carbohydrates 15.9g; fat 6.7g; cholesterol 66.4mg; sodium 146mg.

39 - Double Tomato Bruschetta

Preparation	Cooking	Servings
20 min	**10 min**	**12**

Ingredients:

- 6 roma (plum) tomatoes, chopped
- ½ cup sun-dried tomatoes, packed in oil
- 3 cloves minced garlic
- ¼ cup olive oil
- 2 tablespoons balsamic vinegar
- ¼ cup fresh basil, stems removed

- ¼ teaspoon salt
- ¼ teaspoon ground black pepper
- 1 French baguette
- 2 cups shredded mozzarella cheese

Directions:

1. Preheat the oven on broiler setting.

2. In a large bowl, combine the roma tomatoes, sun-dried tomatoes, garlic, olive oil, vinegar, basil, salt, and pepper. Allow the mixture to sit for 10 minutes.

3. Cut the baguette into 3/4-inch slices. On a baking sheet, arrange the baguette slices in a single layer. Broil for 1 to 2 minutes, until slightly brown.

4. Divide the tomato mixture evenly over the baguette slices. Top the slices with mozzarella cheese.

5. Broil for 5 minutes, or until the cheese is melted.

Nutrition: Calories per serving: 215 calories; protein 9.6g;
carbohydrates 24.8g; fat 8.9g; cholesterol 12.1mg; sodium 425.6mg.

40 - Blackberry Pie

Preparation	Cooking	Servings
10 min	10 min	4

Ingredients:

- 1 vanilla bean, cut lengthwise, deseeded

- ¼ teaspoon cinnamon

- 6 cups blackberry, sliced

- ¼ cup unsweetened coconut milk

- ½ cup orange juice, freshly squeezed

Directions:

1. Combine all your ingredients.

2. In a medium-size skillet on medium-high heat, cook the fruit mixture for 10 minutes.

3. Divide the fruit mixture among four serving dishes.

4. Top with 1 tablespoon of coconut milk.

5. Serve and enjoy!

Nutrition: Calories: 109 Fat: 0.1 g Carbs: 28.5 g Protein: 0.2 g Fiber: 4.5 g

41 – Waffle Vaniglia

Preparation	Cooking	Servings
15 min	**20 min**	**4**

Ingredients:

- 2 egg yolks
- 1 teaspoon vanilla extract
- 1 cup buttermilk
- ¼ cup butter, melted
- 1 cup all-purpose flour
- 1 ½ teaspoons baking powder

- ½ teaspoon baking soda
- ½ tablespoon white sugar
- ¼ teaspoon salt
- 2 egg whites
- 1 pinch ground cinnamon

Directions:

1. Preheat your waffle iron.

2. In a medium bowl, whisk together the eggs, vanilla, buttermilk and butter until well blended. Combine the flour, baking powder, baking soda, sugar, salt and cinnamon; stir into the buttermilk mixture. In a separate bowl, whip the egg whites with an electric mixer until stiff. Fold into the batter.

3. Spoon batter onto the hot waffle iron, close, and cook until golden brown. Waffles are usually done when the steam subsides.

Nutrition: Calories per serving: 380 calories; protein 11.4g; carbohydrates 39.3g; fat 19.4g; cholesterol 180.5mg; sodium 821.4mg

42 - Coconut Puffs

Preparation	Cooking	Servings
10 min	20 min	4

Ingredients:

- ¾ cup all-purpose flour
- ½ cup self-rising flour
- ½ teaspoon ground cinnamon
- ½ teaspoon ground cardamom
- ¼ cup white sugar
- 1 ½ cups coconut milk

- 1 quart oil for frying

Directions:

1. In a medium bowl, mix all-purpose flour, self-rising flour, cinnamon, cardamom and sugar. Stir in coconut milk until lumps disappear.

2. Heat oil in deep-fryer or wok to 375 degrees F (190 degrees C). Drop batter by tablespoons into hot oil. Fry until golden brown. Remove with a slotted spoon and drain on paper towels.

Nutrition: Calories per serving: 552 calories; protein 5.7g; carbohydrates 44.8g; fat 40.5g; sodium 210mg.

43 - Vegan Lemon Poppy Scones

Preparation	Cooking	Servings
15 min	20 min	12

Ingredients:

- 2 cups all-purpose flour
- ¾ cup white sugar
- 4 teaspoons baking powder
- ½ teaspoon salt
- ¾ cup vegan margarine
- 1 lemon, zested and juiced

- 2 tablespoons poppy seeds
- ½ cup soy milk
- ½ cup water

Directions:

1. Preheat the oven to 400 degrees F (200 degrees C). Grease a baking sheet.

2. Sift the flour, sugar, baking powder and salt into a large bowl. Cut in margarine until the mixture is the consistency of large grains of sand. I like to use my hands to rub the margarine into the flour. Stir in poppy seeds, lemon zest and lemon juice. Combine the soy milk and water, and gradually stir into the dry ingredients until the batter is moistened, but still thick like biscuit dough. You may not need all of the liquid.

3. Spoon 1/4 cup sized plops of batter onto the greased baking sheet so they are about 3 inches apart.

4. Bake for 10 to 15 minutes the preheated oven, until golden.

Nutrition: Calories per serving: 240 calories; protein 3g; carbohydrates 30.8g; fat 12.3g; sodium 354.6mg.

44 - Berry Muffins

Preparation	Cooking	Servings
35 min	35 min	12

Ingredients:

- 1 ⅓ cups all-purpose flour
- 1 cup rolled oats
- ¼ cup brown sugar
- 1 tablespoon baking powder
- ½ teaspoon ground cinnamon
- 1 cup milk

- 1 egg, beaten
- 3 tablespoons vegetable oil
- 2 cups fresh blueberries

Directions:

1. Preheat oven to 425 degrees F (220 degrees C). Spray muffin cups with non-stick cooking spray, or use cupcake liners.

2. In a medium-size bowl, combine flour, oats, brown sugar, baking powder, and cinnamon. Stir in milk, egg, and oil. Continue stirring until the mixture is well blended. Fold in the berries. Spoon the mixture into the muffin cups, 2/3 full.

3. Bake 25 to 30 minutes or until light golden brown.

Nutrition: Calories per serving: 155 calories; protein 3.7g; carbohydrates 24.5g; fat 4.9g; cholesterol 17.1mg; sodium 138.3mg.

45 - Vegan Apple Carrot Muffins

Preparation	Cooking	Servings
25 min	**25 min**	**12**

Ingredients:

- 1 cup brown sugar
- ½ cup white sugar
- 2 ½ cups all-purpose flour
- 4 teaspoons baking soda
- 1 teaspoon baking powder
- 4 teaspoons ground cinnamon

- 2 teaspoons salt
- 2 cups finely grated carrots
- 2 large apples - peeled, cored and shredded
- 6 teaspoons egg replacer (dry)
- 1 ¼ cups applesauce
- ¼ cup vegetable oil

Directions:

1. Preheat oven to 375 degrees F (190 degrees C). Grease muffin cups or line with paper muffin liners.

2. In a large bowl combine brown sugar, white sugar, flour, baking soda, baking powder, cinnamon and salt. Stir in carrot and apple; mix well.

3. In a small bowl whisk together egg substitute, applesauce and oil. Stir into dry ingredients.

4. Spoon batter into prepared pans.

5. Bake in preheated oven for 20 minutes. Let muffins cool in pan for 5 minutes before removing from pans to cool completely.

Nutrition: Calories per serving: 257 calories; protein 3.1g; carbohydrates 51.6g; fat 4.9g; sodium 849.7mg.

46 - German Plum Rolls

Preparation	Cooking	Servings
50 min	**60 min**	**12**

Ingredients:

- 1 cup chopped almonds
- 1 ⅓ cups cream cheese
- ½ cup milk
- ½ cup vegetable oil
- 1 pinch salt
- ⅝ cup white sugar

- 1 teaspoon ground cinnamon

- 4 cups all-purpose flour

- ¼ cup baking powder

- ⅞ cup plum butter

- 1 ¾ pounds plums, pitted and diced

- 2 tablespoons butter, melted

Directions:

1. Preheat oven to 350 degrees F (175 degrees C). Lightly grease a 10-inch springform pan.

2. Place a skillet over medium-high heat. Toast the almonds in the hot skillet until they turn brown; set aside to cool.

3. Combine the cream cheese, milk, oil, salt, sugar, and cinnamon in a bowl. Mix in the flour and baking powder; knead together until smooth. Place the dough on a lightly floured surface, and roll the dough into a 20-inch square. Spread the plum butter, plums, and toasted almonds over the dough. Roll the dough up tightly like a jelly roll. Cut into 12 even slices. Arrange rolls in prepared pan. Brush butter over top of the rolls.

4. Bake in preheated oven until golden brown, 40 to 55 minutes.

Nutrition: Calories per serving: 499 calories; protein 8.8g; carbohydrates 62.7g; fat 24.9g; cholesterol 34.3mg; sodium 585.7mg.

47 - Pumpkin Bread

Preparation	Cooking	Servings
20 min	**55 min**	**20**

Ingredients:

- 1 (15 ounce) can pumpkin puree
- 4 eggs
- 1 cup vegetable oil
- ⅔ cup water
- 3 cups white sugar
- 3 ½ cups all-purpose flour

- 2 teaspoons baking soda
- 1 ½ teaspoons salt
- 1 teaspoon ground cinnamon
- 1 teaspoon ground nutmeg
- ½ teaspoon ground cloves
- ¼ teaspoon ground ginger

Directions:

1. Preheat oven to 350 degrees F (175 degrees C). Grease and flour three 7x3 inch loaf pans.

2. In a large bowl, mix together pumpkin puree, eggs, oil, water and sugar until well blended. In a separate bowl, whisk together the flour, baking soda, salt, cinnamon, nutmeg, cloves and ginger. Stir the dry ingredients into the pumpkin mixture until just blended. Pour into the prepared pans.

3. Bake for about 50 minutes in the preheated oven. Loaves are done when toothpick inserted in center comes out clean.

Nutrition: Calories per serving: 263 calories; protein 3.1g; carbohydrates 40.6g; fat 10.3g; cholesterol 31mg; sodium 305.4mg.

48 -Zucchini Bread

Preparation	Cooking	Servings
25 min	55 min	8

Ingredients:

- 3 cups all-purpose flour
- 1 teaspoon salt
- 1 teaspoon baking soda
- 1 teaspoon baking powder
- 1 tablespoon ground cinnamon
- 3 eggs

- 1 cup vegetable oil
- 2 ¼ cups white sugar
- 3 teaspoons vanilla extract
- 2 cups grated zucchini
- 1 cup chopped walnuts

Directions:

1. Grease and flour two 8 x 4 inch pans. Preheat oven to 325 degrees F (165 degrees C).

2. Sift flour, salt, baking powder, soda, and cinnamon together in a bowl.

3. Beat eggs, oil, vanilla, and sugar together in a large bowl. Add sifted ingredients to the creamed mixture, and beat well. Stir in zucchini and nuts until well combined. Pour batter into prepared pans.

4. Bake for 40 to 60 minutes, or until tester inserted in the center comes out clean. Cool in pan on rack for 20 minutes. Remove bread from pan, and completely cool.

Nutrition: Calories per serving: 304 calories; protein 9.4g; carbohydrates 33.8g; fat 16.2g; cholesterol 31.4mg; sodium 69.2mg.

49 - French Toast

Preparation	Cooking	Servings
15 min	25 min	10

Ingredients:

- ¼ cup all-purpose flour
- 1 cup milk
- 1 pinch salt
- 3 eggs
- ½ teaspoon ground cinnamon
- 1 teaspoon vanilla extract

- 1 tablespoon white sugar

- 12 thick slices bread

Directions:

1. Measure flour into a large mixing bowl. Slowly whisk in the milk. Whisk in the salt, eggs, cinnamon, vanilla extract and sugar until smooth.

2. Heat a lightly oiled griddle or frying pan over medium heat.

3. Soak bread slices in mixture until saturated. Cook bread on each side until golden brown. Serve hot.

Nutrition: Calories per serving: 123 calories; protein 4.8g; carbohydrates 19.4g; fat 2.7g; cholesterol 48.1mg; sodium 230.2mg.

50 - Zucchini Home Fries

Preparation	Cooking	Servings
15 min	**20 min**	**4**

Ingredients:

- 4 medium zucchinis

- 1 teaspoon onion powder

- 1 teaspoon of sea salt

- 1 red bell pepper, seeded, diced

- ½ sweet white onion, chopped

- ¼ cup vegetable broth

- ½ cup mushrooms, sliced

Directions:

1.   In a medium-sized microwave-safe bowl, microwave the 4 zucchinis for about 4 minutes or until soft. Allow zucchinis to cool.

2.   Add the broth into a large nonstick pan over medium heat, add the red bell pepper and onion. Sauté your vegetables for 5 minutes.

3.   While the vegetables are cooking, slice your zucchinis into quarters.

4.   Add the mushrooms, onion powder, salt, and zucchinis to the pan. Cook your mixture for about 10 minutes or until the zucchinis are crisp.

5.   Serve and enjoy!

Nutrition: Calories: 337 Fat: 0.8 g Carbs: 74.8 g Protein: 9.3 g Fiber: 12.4 g

Conclusion:

THANK YOU

First of all, thank you for purchasing Vegetarian Recipes Cookbook for Beginners. I know you could have picked any number of books to read, but you chose this book, and for that, I am extremely grateful.

I hope that it added value and quality to your everyday life.

I wish you all the best in your future success!

Amanda Altman

CPSIA information can be obtained
at www.ICGtesting.com
Printed in the USA
BVHW061409250221
601119BV00001B/206